TIME FOR KIDS READERS

by Lisa Trumbauer

Harcourt

Orlando   Austin   Chicago   New York   Toronto   London   San Diego

Visit *The Learning Site!*
www.harcourtschool.com

Polar Bears

Gorillas

Seals

Kangaroos

Elephants

Zoos give animals homes that are like their real homes. A map of the zoo shows you where they live.

3

Gorillas live in the rain forest.

Polar bears live in the Arctic.

Elephants live in the savannas.

Seals live in the ocean.

Many animals live at the zoo!